Seed To Sea
Kumulipo Connections
Volume 1

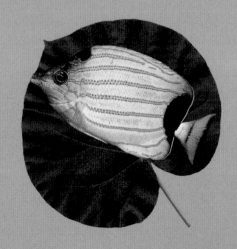

Introduction

This is the first volume of Seed To Sea, Kumulipo Connections: a pairing of six animal and plants found in an ancient Hawaiian creation chant called the Kumulipo. The series delves in to the mysteries of ancient Hawai'i and the way that animals and plants are related in the Kumulipo.

This book comes to you to ignite the fire in your soul to protect the Hawaiian Islands, the creatures that live there, and the oceans surrounding them.

In the Hawaiian Kumulipo, a cosmogonic and genealogical chant, some plants and animals of the land (mauka) have partner species in the sea (makai) or streams (wai). These partner species were chosen by the ancients because of the similarity of their names, how they looked like each other & their uses together medicinally and culturally (some partners are not entirely clear).

For this volume the creatures chosen are easily found in any Hawaiian forest or reef. They represent a natural bridge that enabled a more sustainable way of life from the mountains to the sea: mauka to makai. These plants can also be easily propagated so that we may work to reforest our fragile ecosystem. All the creatures in this book, whether native (endemic or indigenous), or introduced, were used by people in some way in or around the sea: as a food source and offerings to the gods.

Many plants were brought to Hawaii by early Polynesian voyagers. Plants were used to create ocean related tools. These implements helped people to expand their horizons as voyagers sailed around the Hawaiian Archipelago and beyond. The plants that were used in activities like fishing, surfing, healing, and canoe traveling helped people stick together in their daily quest to survive.

It is our responsibility to leave the earth in better shape than when we found it by combining cultural traditions of yesterday with environmental practices of today. Let's encourage children to be a part of their own future by presenting them with culturally acceptable and scientifically proven solutions to the present day problems many communities face. We can plant healthy seeds in our children by involving them with activities like reading books, planting trees, recycling, learning celestial navigation, bird watching, sharing time with the elders (kupuna), fishing, and last but not least - "talking story" (wala'au).

The Hawaiians are tied to the health of the 'aina (land and sea). They have strict rules for preserving and protecting resources. Some of these rules have fallen by the wayside. Many places on land have been protected, but the ocean still needs our help. There can be a balance with fish huggers (those that protect fish and their habitat) & fish hunters (those that eat and collect fish); we can make sure that both habitats and species are preserved for future generations: for our food and enjoyment.

Discover the plants that are used to make sea related implements. You can identify these plants, become familiar with their uses, and plant or propagate these plants. The creatures of the reef can be seen from shore, snorkeling or diving. Learn how to watch these creatures while being safe as you explore the coasts of Hawai'i. Have fun, and give thanks to the Hawaiian ancestors for everything they have discovered, learned and passed down to us. Please malama 'aina (care for the land and the sea) to provide nourishment and tools for our own survival.

There is so much to learn about how "it" is all interconnected. The information here was compiled from many sources. Thorough definitions and a larger number of Hawaiian-English and English-Hawaiian words can be found in Pukui and Elbert's Hawaiian Dictionary or at www.wehewehe.org. Diacritical marks (to assist with pronunciation: 'okina and kahakō) have been inserted to the best of our knowledge and omitted when "print safe" fonts were necessary .

Note on Species Classification: *Native indigenous* - Arrived in Hawai'i without the aid of humans by wind, ocean currents or animals. *Native endemic* - evolved in the Hawaiian Islands (or individual island) from an indigenous species and found nowhere else. *Polynesian Introduction* -brought to the Hawaiian Islands by the early Polynesian settlers. *Post-Contact Introduction*—brought to the Hawaiian Islands after Western contact (1778). *Naturalized*—Not native to the Hawaiian Islands, but now growing wild in the Hawaiian Islands.

Kukui Tree & Pāku'iku'i Fish

209. Hānau ka Pāku'iku'i noho i kai.

The Surgeonfish gives birth, it is found in the sea.

210. Kia'i 'ia e ka lā'au Kukui noho i uka.

Guarded by the Candlenut in the uplands

Hawaiian Name: Kukui

Common Name: Candlenut tree

Scientific Name: *Aleurites moluccana*

Evolutionary Classification: Polynesian Introduction

Habitat: makai (sea), kula (upland), mauka (landward)

Uses on the sea: fishing canoes and canoe parts, dye for lines and tapa cloth, enhanced clarity of water, night torches, varnish for canoes

Other uses: medicinal, laxative, leis, relish ('inamona)

Description: They call me Kukui. Being the state tree of Hawai'i, I can be found easily on

most islands. A grove of my trees give off a white shimmer due to the silvery green color of the underside of my leaves. I am a valuable tree brought over by Polynesian ocean voyagers. I am also called the candle nut tree since the oil in my nut was burned to provide light for the first settlers. I am a very adaptable tree and can thrive in many climates.

Depending on my species, I have two different types of leaves: one resembles a maple leaf from North America, and the other is long and lance shaped.

My nuts are what my tree is known for. They are roundish and green on the tree, and turn black or white upon weathering. Taking a walk on the beach, one can almost always find my

weathered nuts. Pick one up and smell it. Some think my nuts are stinky. The kernels from my nuts are strung on coconut midribs or slivers of bamboo and burned for lights, hence the name "candle nut" tree. Keiki (kids) are then responsible for turning them so the next candle nut will light. Oil from my nuts was also used in stone oil lamps with kapa cloth wicks. I make great torches that enable fishermen to see at night. My nut is chewed and spat on water to create a "lens" so one can see the fish underneath. My bark is put in salt, and boiled for a long time, then lines and nets ('upena) are soaked and stretched so they do not kink and for preservative. This makes a good dye for "hang

stick," an ancient way of fishing. Tattoo dye is made from the soot of my nuts on fire and mixed with coconut water or oil. This dye can be rubbed into surfboards for color by staining and drying. Several coats of my oil can be applied.

In Hawaiʻi I am a symbol of enlightenment, protection and peace. Kukui is considered to be the body form of Kamapuaʻa, the pig god. On the altar of Lono is placed a wooden carving shaped like a pig's head.

In the Kumulipo, an ancient Hawaiian creation chant, my partner species is the pākuʻikuʻi (Achilles tang).

Kukui Tree & Pāku'iku'i Fish

209. Hānau ka Pāku'iku'i noho i kai.

The Surgeonfish gives birth, it is found in the sea.

210. Kia'i 'ia e ka lā'au Kukui noho i uka.

Guarded by the Candlenut in the uplands

Hawaiian Name: Pāku'iku'i

Common Name: Achilles Tang

Common Family Name: Surgeonfish

Scientific Name: *Acanthurus achilles*

Evolutionary Classification: Indigenous

Distribution: Known From Polynesia and Micronesia, also Mexico and islands of the eastern Pacific

Habitat: makai (sea) - on rocky shores and near exposed coral reefs where water moves swiftly through surge channels generally less than 5 m (16 feet). I am very territorial.

Size: to 10 inches (25 cm)

Diet: I eat wispy and delicate leafy algae. Speaking of diet: I was eaten always cooked, and am excellent broiled. Make sure you know which reef fish are safe to eat.

Many algae (seaweed) eaters, such as myself, can make you sick because I eat a toxic algae that builds up in my body. Sometime I have this sickness, and sometimes I don't...It's called ciguatera (*Gamberdiscus spp.*) and scientists are still trying to understand it. It can happen in calm areas and usually more in the summer months. If you ever feel sick after eating a fish please call your state and county officials for assistance.

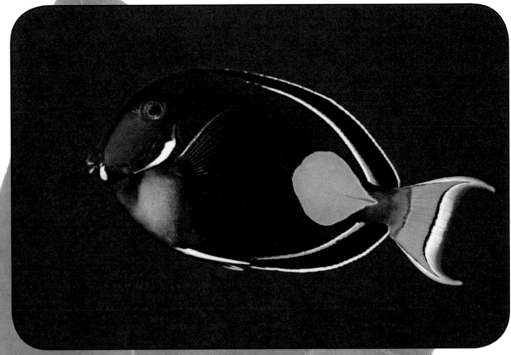

Description: I have a scalpel-like spine (like a sharp knife doctors use in surgery) at the base of my lunate (moon shaped) tail which gives my surgeonfish family its common name.

The brilliant orange marking around my blades act as warning coloration - the bright color highlights my sharp spines. The blades on either side of the tail are modified scales. Each fits into a slot, but can be exposed when I flex my tail. My blades are used both in defense from predators and to ward off food competitors or shelter areas.

My body outline is oval, it is highly compressed from side to side (laterally). I have a small mouth and eyes set high on my head. Sometimes aquarium collectors take me from my home on the reef. You can help me by watching me on the reefs and making sure there are plenty of fish for all to see and eat!

Fish Huggers and Fish Hunters unite.

In the Kumulipo, an ancient Hawaiian creation chant, my partner species is kukui.

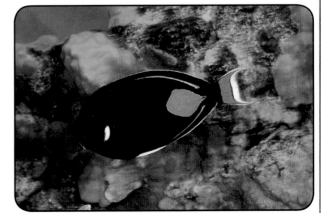

Hau Tree & Pāhau Fish

179. Hānau ka Pāhau noho i kai

The Striped Flatfish gives birth, it is found in the sea

180. Kiaʻi ʻia e ka Lau Hau noho i uka

Guarded by the Leaf of the Hau in the uplands

Hawaiian Name: Hau

Common Name: Sea Hibiscus

Scientific Name: *Talipariti tiliaceus*

Evolutionary Classification: Native - Indigenous, and probably brought by early Polynesians

Habitat: near rivers and brackish waters, makai (sea), mauka (upland)

Uses on the sea: cordage, twine and rope for fishing nets, fishing lines, wood for outrigger floats, crossbeams (ʻiakos) on canoes, shark nooses

Other uses: Firewood and fire starting, adz (ax) handles, brooms, tapa cloth, medicinal

Parts used: wood, fibers

Description: My common name is Hau. I probably arrived by ocean currents to the Hawaiian Islands. My wood is very buoyant; it floats and travels well.

I am now recognized as indigenous due to a recent discovery of one of my leaf imprints found in a stone giving insight to archaeologists as to my date of arrival.

I was definitely introduced, by way of boat, from Polynesian settlers. One can almost always find me growing where the rivers and the sea meet in brackish waters. I love water and love to climb over it. I can form amazing lush canopies over water. My flowers are mostly yellow and turn orange towards sunset. One cannot miss my large heart shaped green leaves. Traveling through my twisty, woody branches can surely test ones climbing skills. Lower elevations are my favorite, because I do not like being too far from my friend, the ocean. The Tahitians believe that I am the grandchild of heaven and earth. My greatest strength is in my fibers, which are turned into durable cordage. I trap sharks in my nets. Fishermen like my wood for outrigger floats, and 'iako (crossbeams pronounced "yaku") on canoes. Traditionally, my branches were piled near the shoreline to indicate fishing was kapu (off limits), because spawning was occurring in that area. We can protect fish by letting their babies grow big. Many consider me an invasive plant because I can dominate an area very quickly, so take care if you plant me. One Hawai`i legend says that hau is a sister of the goddess Hina, that changed into a tree.

In the Kumulipo, an ancient Hawaiian creation chant, my partner species is the pāhau (butterflyfish).

Hau Tree & Pāhau Fish

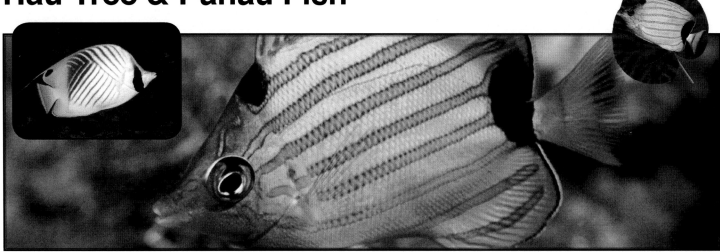

179. Hānau ka Pāhau noho i kai

The Striped Flatfish gives birth, it is found in the sea

180. Kiaʻi ʻia e ka Lau Hau noho i uka

Guarded by the Leaf of the Hau in the uplands

Hawaiian Name: Lauhau, also known as kikakapu and pāhau

Common Name: Bluestriped & Threadfin Butterflyfish

Common Family Name: Butterflyfish

Scientific Name: *Chaetodon fremblii* and *Chaetodon auriga*

Evolutionary Classification: Bluestriped = endemic & Threadfin = indigenous

Distribution: Bluestriped = endemic - "a relic"; no other close relatives in the Indo-Pacific; Threadfin = Indo-Pacific Region.

Habitat: I live in shallow water over coral reefs with crevices and ledges. I occasionally visit distant parts of the reef, but always return home to my part of the reef, where I live for my entire life (8-10 years).

Size: to 15 & 20 cm.

Diet: We are omnivores; we eat coral polyps, tentacles of tube worms, polychaete worms, sponges, filamentous algae, eggs and other small invertebrates (creatures without backbones). Speaking of diet: Some say, I am "bony, not worth eating" while others say "sweet flesh, broiled on charcoal immediately, without scaling or cleaning."

I am also a "bait nibbler"; if you like to pole fish you have seen me try to eat your bait.

Description: Blue stripes, delicate, colorful, and highly maneuverable. From the front, my body is thin; this helps me move quickly through narrow spaces. From the side you can see that I have an oval, hau leaf shaped body and a narrow long mouth. I am diurnal (I swim and eat in the day and rest in reef crevices and under ledges at night). I am yellow with seven blue stripes; three of these stripes meet at my eye. I have a large black spot on top of my head where my dorsal (top) fin starts and a black bar on the base of my tail. I have a harem as large as four females and I spawn (lay eggs) before the week before the full moon in February and March just before sunset.

*Note: Some say that the pahau, the "striped flatfish" is an old lauhau fish. Most say that lauhau is either the fourspot, threadfin, bluestriped or teardrop butterflyfish, The the pahau is yellow-grey like an old grey hau leaf (possible night or terminal coloration)... eaten raw, salted or pulehu (broiled) with maikoiko and hinalea fish after being wrapped in ti leaves. Fish names vary from place to place in Hawai'i; and hybrids occur. Some names have changed as cultures meld and oral knowledge has been forgotten. Please support Hawaiian cultural resurgence.

In the Kumulipo, an ancient Hawaiian creation chant, my partner species is hau.

Hala Tree & Pahaha Fish

173. Hānau ka Pahaha noho i kai

The Mullet gives birth, it is found in the sea

174. Kiaʻi ʻia e ka Pūhala noho i uka

Guarded by the Pandanus in the uplands

Hawaiian Name: Hala

Common Name: Screw Pine, Tourist Pineapple,

Hawaiian Name: Hala, Pūhala.

Scientific Name: *Pandanus tectorius*

Evolutionary Classification: Native - Indigenous, and probably brought by early Polynesians

Habitat: makai (sea), kula (upland)

Parts used: leaves, wood, fruits, flowers

Uses on the sea: sails, matting to protect baggage and keep paddlers dry, canoe paint and waterproofing made from ashes of lauʻhala mixed with other plants, and canoe rollers

Other uses: leeping and floor mats, baskets, fans, thatching, house timbers, leis, medicinal flowers and root tips, and food during famine

Description: They call me Hala. I am one tree you will surely find easily near the ocean, due to my most unique appearance of "teepee like" aerial roots (ule hala) and long, wild, green, and brown spiny leaves (lau hala) that hang crooked or blow in the wind.

I can grow right next to the sea, tolerating salty sea spray and harsh winds. I produce fruit that resembles a pineapple on my female trees and white flowers on my male trees called hinano. I love

to grow in groups. My fruit is edible although not commonly eaten and considered "famine food". I grow in many places throughout the Pacific islands such as the Philippines, Australia, Melanesia, and Java. I am definitely not endangered. I am almost as common as coconut trees are in the islands. I can grow almost anywhere in a tropical climate although I prefer lower elevations. My leaves are woven into sails for canoes, mats, baskets, fans and more! My flowers and root tips have medicinal qualities. After careful propagation of my seeds, I am easy to take care of.

In the Kumulipo, an ancient Hawaiian creation chant, my partner species is the pahaha (mullet).

Hala Tree & Pahaha Fish

173. Hānau ka Pahaha noho i kai

The Mullet gives birth, it is found in the sea

174. Kiaʻi ʻia e ka Pūhala noho i uka

Guarded by the Pandanus in the uplands

Hawaiian Name: Pahaha

Common Name: Mullet

Common Family Name: Mullet

Scientific Name: *Mugil cephalus*

Evolutionary Classification: Indigenous

Habitat: makai (sea), kula (upland)

Distribution: I can be found worldwide in warm tropical seas.

Habitat: You can find me swimming with my friends in school in shallow, often brackish (mixture of salt and fresh water) coastal waters and I am easily raised in fishponds

Size: to about 20 inches (30+ cm)

Diet: I am a bottom feeder, and open my mouth and take in sand, algae, or mud and then filter out the "goodies" through my gills and eat it. Sometimes I eat phytoplankton, zooplankton, small benthic crustaceans or worms. I have very small teeth. Speaking of diet: I can be eaten raw with limu (algae) manauea (*Gracliaria sp.*) and limu ʻoʻolu (*Champia parvula*); and sometimes broiled or baked in ti or ginger leaves, and also dried.

Description: I am one of the early Hawaiians' most important freshwater or brackish food fishes. I am often raised in captivity in Hawai'i now and in the past. I have a flattened head, blunt snout, and am colored silvery bluish gray. My long body is rounded or oval with large scales and two well-separated dorsal fins (top). I escape from predators and fishing nets by leaping and jumping out of the water.

In the Kumulipo, an ancient Hawaiian creation chant, my partner species is hala.

'Awa Plant & 'A'awa Fish

239. Hānau ka 'A'awa noho i kai

The Wrasse gives birth, it is found in the sea

240. Kia'i 'ia e ka 'Awa noho i uka

Guarded by the Kava in the uplands

Hawaiian Name: 'Awa

Common Name: Kava

Scientific Name: *Piper methysticum*

Evolutionary Classification: Polynesian Introduction

Habitat: forest edges, near streamlets, damp uplands

Parts used: all parts of the plant, especially the root

Uses on the sea: seasickness, relieve soreness from paddling

Other uses: medicinal - headaches, asthma, stomachaches, relaxing potion, and as an offering to gods

Description: Take a drink and feel no pain - 'awa is my name. I am most likely to be found at forest edges, near streams, and damp shaded valleys. I am primarily propagated by plant growers. It takes two to three years until my roots are ready for harvest. A relaxing potion is made from my roots. It is commonly given as an offering to the gods and the aumakua (personal god) of the family. I am sometimes planted near taro. Fishermen drink me to relieve soreness from paddling.

I have green heart shaped leaves with tubular stalks and swellings called nodes that emerge from my woody rootstalk. I advise you not to drink my potion if you are pregnant or lactating.

In the Kumulipo, an ancient Hawaiian creation chant, my partner species is the 'a'awa (Hawaiian hog fish).

'Awa plant & 'A'awa Fish

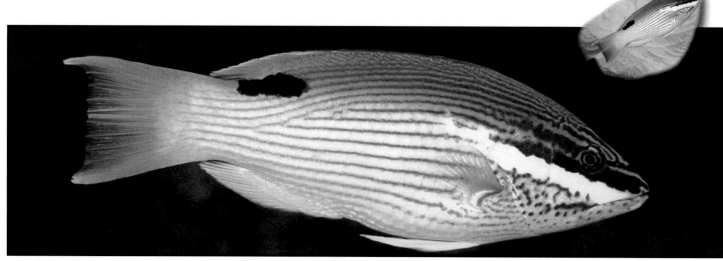

239. Hānau ka 'A'awa noho i kai

The Wrasse gives birth, it is found in the sea

240. Kia'i 'ia e ka 'Awa noho i uka

Guarded by the Kava in the uplands

Hawaiian Name: 'A'awa

Common Name: Hawaiian hogfish

Common Family Name: Wrasse

Scientific Name: *Bodianus albotaeniatus*

Evolutionary Classification: Endemic

Distribution: Hawaiian Islands and Johnston Island

Habitat: You can find me around the coral reefs of Hawai'i. I am diurnal (active by day), so you may see me eating in the daytime. Sometimes at night I like to hide and bury myself in the sand.

Size: to 20 inches (50 cm)

Diet: I am carnivorous (meat-eating), and I feed on a variety of mollusks and crustaceans but also eat sea urchins, crabs, brittlestars, and occasionally small fishes. As a young fish, I clean other reef fishes. Speaking of diet: My white flesh can be eaten broiled or dried. Sometimes I am a pupu (snack), eaten after drinking 'awa, as an aftertaste.

Description: As a juvenile I have a white tail and mostly black body with bright yellow on the upper head and back. As I mature, the yellow fades and the black recedes into a saddle-like spot under my dorsal fin (top), leaving my body looking pale with dark streaks on my head and many fine lines running down the length of my body. A long white mark under my eye gives me my scientific name, which means "white ribbon." In some areas of Hawai'i I am over fished (too many are taken and none come back).

In the Kumulipo, an ancient Hawaiian creation chant, my partner species is 'awa.

Milo Tree & Laumilo Eel

215. Hānau ka Laumilo noho i kai

The Eel gives birth, it is found in the sea

216. Kiaʻi ʻia e ka lāʻau Milo noho i uka

Guarded by the Milo in the uplands

Hawaiian Name: Milo

Common Name: Milo

Scientific Name: *Thespesia populnea*

Evolutionary Classification: Native - Indigenous, and probably brought by early Polynesians

Parts used: all parts of plant, especially the root

Habitat: Coastal areas, low lying plains in makai (ocean) region

Uses on the sea: Paddles, and ama (outrigger floats)

Other uses: Food bowls, cutting boards, crafts

Description: Milo is my name, wood is my game. My trunks grow curvy when old, and straight up and down when young. It's fun to climb me when I'm old, because my branches are curvy and can be low to the ground. My outer bark is grey, ridgy and layered. It can easily be torn off.

I can easily be made into bowls and canoe paddles by wood carvers. My inner bark is mixed colors of reddish brown, tan, and brown. I am durable enough to last a long time, but light enough to lift and be used on an outrigger ama (canoe side floats). My leaves are green and heart shaped. My shoots grow right out of my trunks and my branches are green. I have many leaves that grow in an alternate pattern with alternate veins. If you touch my leaves, they are soft and pliable. I have clove or acorn shaped seed pods that are green when new and brown when old. They are filled with many seeds.

Look at the seed pods at the ends of my branches. They have about a two inch skinny, woody stem. I have many branches that extend out from my trunk and can range in six inch diameter to about two and a half feet. You can find me by the ocean and rivers. I also can grow inland. I am very tolerant of wind and salty ocean spray. I can even grow right out of the sand. I am abundant and easily found in the Kai and low lying plains of the Hawaiian Islands, Tahiti, and some mainland states. I was especially treasured for my wood in the olden times for making food bowls and cutlery because my wood does not have a strong taste or smell. I was also favored for canoe outrigger parts because I am light weight.

In the Kumulipo, an ancient Hawaiian creation chant, my partner species is the laumilo (undulated moray eel).

Milo Tree & Laumilo Eel

215. Hānau ka Laumilo noho i kai

The Eel gives birth, it is found in the sea

216. Kiaʻi ʻia e ka lāʻau Milo noho i uka

Guarded by the Milo in the uplands

Hawaiian Name: Laumilo

Common Name: Undulated Moray Eel

Common Family Name: Moray Eels

Scientific Name: *Gymnothorax undulatus*

Evolutionary Classification: Indigenous (some eels are endemic)

Habitat: I like lurking in holes and crevices in rocky areas or on the coral reef. During the day, often only my head is visible at the entrance to my shelter, but most of the time you will never see me. I am a dweller of the night, searching within and over the reef for prey that I find with my keen sense of smell. I will often prey on diurnal (day time) species when they are sleeping and resting within the reef at night.

Size: to 3½ feet

Diet: I am a carnivore (meat eater). I eat reef fishes and soft-bodied invertebrates (no backbones) like octopus. Speaking of diet: I was highly prized for food in old Hawaiʻi. Chiefs were fond of me and served me to beloved guests. I, and other Large eels like me, eat lots of algae eating fish.

The fish I eat often contain ciguatera and it builds up in my body, so be aware if eating me: I can be toxic.

Description: My head is long, and I have tube-like nostrils. I ominously open and close my mouth to pump water over my gills. This scares many snorkelers since it looks like I want to bite them. I have a narrow jaw that is full of sharp teeth, including a row down the center of my mouth. My body might be dark brown with light speckles and a net or chain-link fence pattern. I might also look the opposite – almost white with

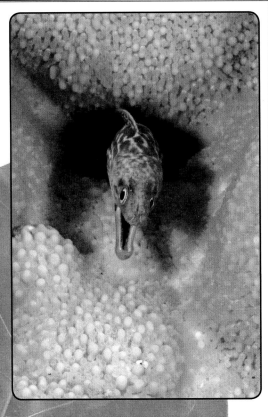

irregular brown blotches. The top of my head often has a greenish-yellow tinge. I swim by moving my entire body side to side in a S-shaped wave. Using this wave pattern I can move forward or backward, an important advantage, since I like living within the narrow holes of the reef. I am one of the most common moray eels, and also one of the meanest. Called "especially vicious"; I would not try to play with me or feed me - if I were you. Some morays have venom also. Hawaiʻi is well known for the abundance of eels here because of few predator species.

In the Kumulipo, an ancient Hawaiian creation chant, my partner species is the milo.

Wauke Tree & Weke Fish

233. Hanau ka Weke noho i kai

The Mullidae gives birth, it is found in the sea

234. Kia'i 'ia ka Wauke noho i uka

Guarded by the Paper Mulberry in the uplands

Hawaiian Name: Wauke

Common Name: Paper Mulberry

Scientific Name: *Broussonetia papyrifera*

Evolutionary Classification: Polynesian Introduction

Parts used: Wood, Stalks, inner bark

Habitat: Near water and taro ponds, sheltered valleys: Mauka and Makai

Uses on the sea: Fish nets, cordage, paddles

Other uses: Tapa (Hawaiian cloth), medicinal properties in the ash and leaf

Description: Aloha! My name is Wauke. My roots were brought over by boat from Polynesia so that I could be propagated in the Hawaiian islands. The main reason people like me so much is that I make great cloth and clothes from my inner fibers. In a place where there are no furry animals to make yarn and fabric with, I am the best resource people have to make clothes from.

Tapa "cloth making" is a very long process that involves pressing, beating, fermenting and soaking my fibers. Historically, everything except the harvest is done by women.

On the ocean, I am valued for my light and buoyant inner bark. I am made into cordage for nets of all kinds: fish nets called upena & carrying nets called koko, from which to hang calabashes of wood and gourds.

If you come looking for me in the wild, you might not find a

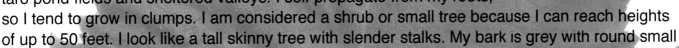

me. I was so popular and essential to the early Polynesians that I was cultivated and harvested on demand. With the passing of time and the arrival of new fabrics and materials there was a drastic decline in the need for my use. I love to be by water and was often planted by taro pond fields and sheltered valleys. I self propagate from my roots, so I tend to grow in clumps. I am considered a shrub or small tree because I can reach heights of up to 50 feet. I look like a tall skinny tree with slender stalks. My bark is grey with round small

knobs. Cultivators cut off my branches so I grow straight up and down. They also keep me at a height of about 9 feet so they can harvest me easily. My leaves umbrella out at the top of my stalks and are rough and ridgy. My leaves are woolly, dark green and scratchy on the top side. Underneath of my leaf, I am mint green and soft. If you break my leaf open a milky white sap will ooze out. I have zigzag ridges on the edges of my leafs and they can be about 3-8 inches across and 4-10 inches tall. I hope you will replant me and learn how to make some Tapa or some cordage from my fibers. Remember I will grow better if I am by water and protected from wind.

In the Kumulipo, an ancient Hawaiian creation chant, my partner species is the weke (goat fish).

Wauke Tree & Weke Fish

233. Hanau ka Weke noho i kai

The Mullidae gives birth, it is found in the sea

234. Kiaʻi ʻia ka Wauke noho i uka

Guarded by the Paper Mulberry in the uplands

Hawaiian Name: Weke

Common Name: Yellowstripe Goatfish

Common Family Name: Goatfishes

Scientific Name: *Mulloidichthys flavolineatus*

Evolutionary Classification: Indigenous (some goatfish are endemic)

Distribution: Indo-Pacific to the Red Sea and East Coast of Africa to the Hawaiian Islands and Pitcairn Islands; and West Pacific from the Ryukyu Islands to southern New South Wales

Habitat: During the day I usually hang out at predictable spots on the reef, either hovering in midwater or lying on the sand. Sometimes I will go into the brackish (mixture of salt and fresh) water.

Size: to 16 inches

Diet: I am carnivorous. I like to feed all of the time – both day and at night, but I have no teeth on the top of my mouth. One can easily spot me by my barbels: chemical sensors that look like a goat's beard. I use

them to busily "taste" the sand for worms, mollusks, and other invertebrates (no backbone). I even use my barbels to flush out shrimp, crabs, or even fish from crevices in the reef. Other fish, like jacks and wrasses, follow me looking for food as I stir up the sand. When I am not feeding, I tuck my barbels out of sight.

Speaking of diet: I am sometimes eaten by people raw, but usually broiled in ti leaves over hot coals. 'Oama (young weke) are eaten eater raw after being salted for a few minutes or dried. Some weke (weke pahalu) can cause "delirium and nightmares" by eating the head or brain. Use caution!

Description: There are many goatfish on the Hawaiian reef. You can easily recognize me, the yellowstripe goatfish, by the squarish black spot on my side that is embedded within a yellow stripe running from my head to my tail. My black spot is often more intense while I am feeding, and it may fade or disappear when I am resting or swimming around with my school. My yellow stripe may also fade. My snout is pointed and my mouth sometimes sticks out. I have a forked tail and two dorsal (top) fins. I was used as offerings to the gods: red weke for certain occasions and white weke for others.

In the Kumulipo, an ancient Hawaiian creation chant, my partner species is the wauke.

Works Cited:

Bornhorst, Heidi Leianuenue. Growing Native Hawaiian Plants: a How-to Guide for the Gardener. Honolulu, Hawaii: Bess, 1996. Print.

Edith Kanaka'ole Foundation. Hilo, Hawai'i: Edith Kanaka'ole Foundation, 2003. Print.

Greenway, Theresa. A Guide To Plant Classification And Plant Biodiversity. Austin: Raintree Steck-Vaughn, 2000. Print.

Hang Stick. Kauai , HI Public Library. Videocassette.

Harrington, Daniel. Hawaiian Encyclopedia: A Comprehensive Guide To The Hawaiian Islands History, Culture, Native Species, Science. 08 Aug. 2010 <www.hawaiianencyclopedia.com>

HawaiiHistory.org - Hawaii History. Web. 21 Apr. 2010. <http://www.hawaiihistory.org>.

Holmes, Tommy. The Hawaiian Canoe. Honolulu: Editions Limited, 1981. Print.

Johnson, Rubellite Kawena. Kumulipo. 1981. Print.

Kepler, Angela Kay. Hawaiian Heritage Plants. Honolulu: University of Hawai'i, 1998. Print.

Kolomona, Solomon. "Old Hawaii." Personal interview.

Krauss, Beatrice H. Plants in Hawaiian Culture. Honolulu: University of Hawaii, 1993. Print.

"Kukui." Canoe Plants of Ancient Hawaii. Web. 22 Feb. 21010. <http://canoeplants.com/kukui.html>.

Lamb, Samuel H. Native Trees And Shrubs Of The Hawaiian Islands. Santa Fe: Sunstone, 1981. Print.

Liliuokalani. The Kumulipo: an Hawaiian Creation Myth. Kentfield, Calif.: Pueo, 1978. Print.

Lilleeng-Rosenberger, Kerin E. Growing Hawai'i's Native Plants: a Simple Step-by-step Approach for Every Species. Honolulu, Hawai'i: Mutual Pub., 2005. Print.

Lilleeng-Rosenberger, Kerin E. "Native Plants." Personal interview.

Lucas, Lois. Plants of Old Hawaii. Honolulu: Bess, 1983. Print.

Nirav, Shunyam. Hawaiian Growing Guide. Kahului: New Dawn, 1995. Print.

"Pandanus Tectorius (Hala)." University of Hawaii. Web. 21 Apr. 2010. <http://www2.hawaii.edu/~eherring/hawnprop/pan-tect.htm>.

Perlman, Steve. "Kauai's' Native Plants On Location." Personal interview.

Randall, John E. Reef and Shore Fishes of the Hawaiian Islands. Honolulu: University of Hawaii Sea Grant College, 2007. Print.

Scott, Susan. Plants And Animals Of Old Hawaii. Honolulu: Bess Inc, 1997. Print.

Stender, Keoki & Yuko. Marine LIfe Photography 06 Aug. 2010. <www.marinelifephotography.com>

Titcomb, Margaret. 1996. Native Use of Fish In Hawaii. University of Hawaii Press: Honolulu, HI

Wagner, W.L., Herbst, D.R., and Sohmer, S.H.: University of Hawai'i Press; Bishop Museum Press, 1999.

Wagner, Warren L., and Herbst, Derral R. Electronic Supplement to the Manual of the Flowering Plants of Hawai'i.

Walther, Michael. A Guide to Hawai'i's Coastal Plants. Honolulu, HI: Mutual Pub., 2004. Print.

Williams, Julie Stewart. From The Mountains To The Sea. Honolulu: Kamehameha, 1997. Print.

Wood, Paul. Tropical Trees Of Hawaii. Waipahu: Island Heritage, 2004. Print.

Thanks to:

www.SaveOurSeas.us

www.MarineLifePhotography.com

www.EarthSurge.com & www.Princeville.biz

www.packyourtrash.org & www.packyourbutts.com

Artists: Kimberly Kirk-cover; Joy Hope-waterwwfall and plants; Viren Olsen-plants

Editors and Writers: Patti Hawkinson, Jenna Hinton, Dharma Wease, SeaLove

National Tropical Botanical Garden– Limahuli Garden and Preserve, Allerton Garden, McBryde Garden.

www.NTBG.org

Kawika Winter - NTBG Limahuli

Roger and Susanne Blum, Alma Valviejaumalla, Sol Kolomona, Fredie Ramos, Steve Palmer, Kerin

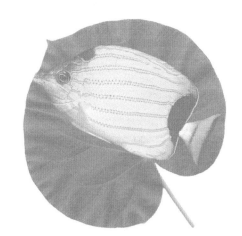

Seed To Sea
Kumulipo Connections
Volume 1

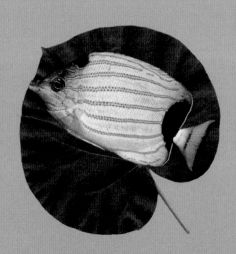

Made in the USA
Monee, IL
12 December 2019